Curtain Call

First published in Republic of Ireland in 2007 by
Trocadero Restaurant in aid of the Irish Cancer Society

Trocadero Restaurant
4 Saint Andrew Street Dublin 2 Ireland
+353 (0)1 677 5545
www.trocadero.ie

Produced by Red Door Project Management
Edited by Melanie Morris
Designed by DCOY
Printed by DCKEbrook
Paper by Swan Paper

ISBN 978-0-9557245-0-3

CURTAIN
CALL

TROCADERO celebrates Irish Theatre

Supporting the Irish Cancer Society
Free Nationwide Nursing Service

irish cancer society

 irish cancer society

FROM THE IRISH CANCER SOCIETY

JOHN McCORMACK

Many people have never cared for a seriously ill person at home and this can cause immense stress as they may not know what to expect. The Irish Cancer Society's free night nursing service helps to reduce this worry for patients and their carers by offering expert care, support and advice at this crucial time.

In the words of Tricia Dorgan, Fermoy, Co Cork: "In August 2005, night nurse Eileen Crosby came to our home to help me take care of my husband Liam. Eileen had a huge impact on our family. She knew all of Liam's medication requirements and that first evening, told me to go upstairs, close the door and have a good night's sleep. My family and I could trust Eileen totally and Liam and Eileen became great friends over many late-night cups of tea."

In 2006 the Society's night nurses provided 4,782 nights of care, looking after 1,283 people with cancer and their families across Ireland. In 2007, almost 5,000 nights of care will be provided. The numbers of people with cancer and their families who are using the service has increased steadily over the years, indicating that more people are choosing to stay at home where feasible, which places increased demands on the service.

Providing a night nurse in a patient's home costs approximately €250 per night, so the Irish Cancer Society must raise about €1.25 million to continue to provide this service in 2007. Thus, we are incredibly grateful that Trocadero has nominated the Society, and in particular, our night nursing programme as the beneficiary of the sales of this book. This will enable more people living in Ireland the opportunity to spend the last few weeks of their lives at home, surrounded by their friends and family.

We wish the much-loved Trocadero well with this venture, and continued success and happiness to Rhona, Robert, Patricia and all the team over the years to come.

John McCormack

John McCormack
Chief Executive

Irish Cancer Society
43-45 Northumberland Road
Dublin 4 Ireland
+353 (0)1 231 0500
1 800 200 700 (National Cancer Helpline)
www.cancer.ie

TROCADERO

A FEAST FOR THE SENSES

BRENDAN KENNELLY

The Trocadero, alias The Troc, has been a centre of fun, craic, delightful conversations, interesting people and jolly good food for me for almost 50 years. That splendid fare is served by some of the most charmingly efficient people you could hope to meet in any top-class restaurant anywhere in the world. The combination of excellent food and brilliant staff has been, and remains, what helps to make The Troc unique.

Just look at it today. What a pleasure it is to stroll into this welcoming place and be greeted by Robert Doggett, an elegant, eloquent, humorous, humane, wise and witty host. And he is helped in so many ways by smiling staff, led by Patricia Aitchison and overseen by the beautiful dynamo, Rhona Teehan. This is The Troc team, the people who make a crucial contribution to customers' enjoyment, pleasure and satisfaction. That Troc team creates an atmosphere of warm welcome and sustained attention throughout any entire evening so that a customer leaves the place feeling, yes, happy.

The actual physical place is itself fascinating, even magnetic. Sit at a table, look around for a while, concentrate on the pictures and photographs on the walls, and you begin to feel that you are part of a journey through the cultural, artistic, theatrical history of Dublin. It is as though these famous figures form a kind of cultural family who are contributing to that warm welcome you feel when you step inside the door. A comfortably seated observer travels back in time while enjoying the finest contemporary food. History becomes a companion.

The Troc has extended in recent years. As I see it, there are now five different sections, including a bar, and each section has a distinct personality while at the same time contributing to the restaurant's overall unique character. Sometimes when restaurants are extended, that overall character tends to become oddly and adversely affected. Not so with The Troc today. It is more Troc than ever.

Now and then, when friends visit me from abroad, I take them to The Troc. They love it. They tend to express the wish to visit the place again. And why wouldn't they? The Troc is unfailingly joyful. Every time I go there, it seems as if it is for the first time. After almost 50 years, that feeling is invigoratingly fresh and rare.

In this age of pressure and stress come to The Troc and taste happiness.

Brendan Kennelly

Brendan Kennelly

TROCADERO
A WORLD OF ITS OWN

"It's 2.40am. Just waiting on a cab. Another great night. See you later. Down to last few bottles of Barolo, are there more coming in? Last sole went at 9.30pm, can you make sure there is plenty for tonight?"

There is always a note for Patricia Aitchison when she arrives at The Trocadero each morning. Left just a few hours earlier by Robert Doggett the Trocadero's esteemed Director Manager. Covering everything and anything, they are like the notes left in a busy household.

The Trocadero is far more than a restaurant, it's been a favourite meeting place for 50 years. Renowned in theatre and media circles, The Troc's first owner Eddie Michaels or Eddie the Greek as he was known, started the tradition of hanging signed photographs of the restaurant's famous, and infamous, patrons on the rich red walls. To this day the photographs continue to accumulate.

The personalities of Rhona, Patricia and Robert reflect the dedication and loyalty of all the staff, the faces of some of whom are as intrinsic to The Troc as the photos that line the walls.

Rhona, already established in business with Kilmartins Wine Bar on Baggot Street and Suesey Street nightclub on Leeson Street acquired The Troc over the whirlwind Christmas of 1984. "When Tom Farrington rang me and asked if I was interested in The Troc, I didn't ask any questions, I just said yes. It was madness. It was my first Christmas in Suesey Street. Patricia was running Kilmartins on her own…" The two friends and associates embarked on a rollercoaster ride.

Robert's journey to front of house was more scenic. Starting as a chef and then working as a waiter on

> **A restaurant with a heart, in the centre of Dublin, The Trocadero nourishes the soul as well as feeding all those who step inside. From generation to generation, The Troc is shorthand for hospitality in the greatest of traditions."**

his nights off from the kitchen, he quickly became the leading man at The Troc. It was through Robert that the restaurant truly took on its identity as a home away from home of Ireland's theatre crowd, a communal greenroom and a perfect place to eat and unwind after a show.

There are countless tales from The Troc, birthdays, weddings and graduations celebrated, opening nights enjoyed and awards toasted. Just as everyone has their favourite table, they all have their own stories of their Trocadero. Deals have been sealed over the famous sole on the bone, beards set alight by the (no longer flaming) sambuca, and hundreds of first dates have been played out under the warm glow of the Tiffany chandeliers.

The restaurant has grown up over the years. While regulars might say that it hasn't changed a bit, there have been ongoing improvements, under the supervision of skilled interior designer Dymphna

Healy, which have maintained the integrity of the old Georgian house. The extended bar with its dramatic lighting has become a favoured place for aperitifs and after dinner drinks; the bevelled mirrors reflect gentle light which spills from handpainted bulbs; and the brass rails, red velvet banquettes and Art Deco details are a homage to the world of theatre which has such close links to The Troc. It is no wonder that Robert calls the start of the evening "Curtain Up".

A restaurant with a heart at the centre of Dublin, The Trocadero nourishes the soul as well as feeding those who step inside. Trocadero is a Dublin tradition as integral and long lasting as the theatre.

"...It's 2.40am. Just waiting on a cab. Another great night. See you later."

ROSALEEN LINEHAN

"It's an odd life pretending to be somebody else. Sometimes it's a great relief (a nice stylish comedy), sometimes it's a bit wearisome (a not so stylish tragedy). Above all, I enjoy the routine and my fellow workers. The big bonus is a lively audience. Good friends and a few glasses of wine after the performance, that's good. Who'd be without it?"

DES KEOGH

"Some of my most enduring and rewarding friendships have been with formidable women of the theatre, in particular Phyllis Ryan, Anna Manahan and Rosaleen Linehan. I met Rosaleen while at UCD and we've survived ever since. In fact, I think I'll probably be remembered for being married to her... Which I'm not!"

BRENDA FRICKER

"I will always remember The Trocadero for their loyalty. They gave me a little party when I won the Oscar. Show business is full of people who understand emotions – more than most amadáns anyhow. And there are so many great writers. I particularly like Shakespeare, he 'gets' women. Should my last supper be at The Troc, I'd like it to start with a dance on the tabletop with Robert and Frank, and a pint of Guinness with a huge head on it."

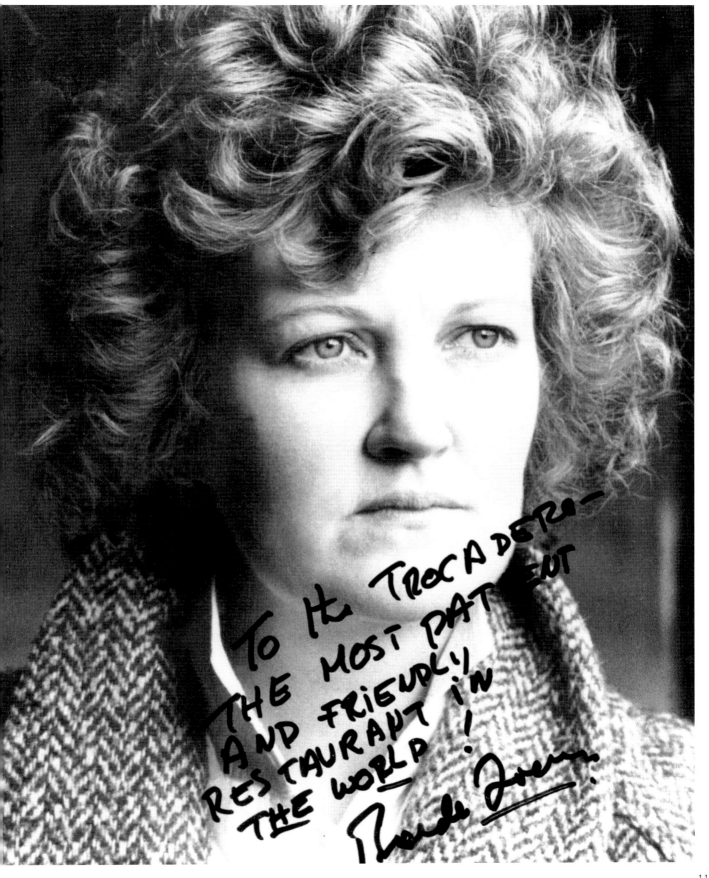

To th Trocadero-
THE MOST PATIENT
AND FRIENDLY
RESTAURANT IN
THE WORLD!

11

DON WYCHERLEY

"I became aware of The Troc when I was working as a bouncer in
Suesey Street, the popular Leeson Street nightclub. Rhona Teehan
owned both and there was always a good rapport between the staff
of each as we'd share postmortems of our respective nights over
port. This was when I first met Robert, and of course, my future wife,
Deirdre who was also working for Rhona at the time. Having plucked
up the courage to ask her out, I decided The Troc would be the
perfect place, not just for the ambience, and the fact that we knew
everyone, but also because we got a staff discount – making things
far more palatable for a doorman/would-be-actor. We've enjoyed
many nights since, and though we've lost our staff discount, The Troc
hasn't lost any of its charm."

PETER O'BRIEN

In a world where a sense of humour can be as rare as an international fashion editor not dressed in black, I have always been attracted to those in the business who don't take it, or themselves, too seriously; a perfect example being my dear friend, stylist Catherine Condell, who celebrated a significant birthday in The Trocadero recently. In Paris, where costume budgets are always big, backstage usually resembles a crowd scene from a Cecil B DeMille movie with armies of dressers, pressers, hair people, make-up people, PR people, boyfriends, girlfriends, caterers and usually me paralysed in a corner, of no use to anybody. I love Wilde, for the language and for his lampooning of upper class snobs while appearing to flatter them – *The Importance of Being Ernest* must surely be the most indestructible play in the English language. I owe a lot to the Gate where I got to do my first costumes with the legendary Joy Gleeson, but I am happiest sitting in a darkened theatre, listening to the overture of some piece of musical theatre yes, I know, the uncoolest thing in the world!"

OM HICKEY

"e are three key people who I regard as having the most influer
y career – Deirdre O'Connell, my tutor in the Stanislavsky met
e Gibson from RTE, and the great playwright Tom MacIntyre, w
ard as the most adventurous and daring of today's great Irish
rs. I've acted, collaborated on and directed a variety of his wo
The Great Hunger is a particular favourite. The Abbey Theatre i
ue and historic place. It is obliged to have beautiful, savage ar
ersive conversations with the Irish nation. This is not always th
but I have been fortunate to be part of these dialogues since
970s. I have been inspired and enthralled by many wonderful
ormances, like Donal McCann in Brian Friel's *The Faith Healer,*
Blakely in *Morning After Optimism* by Tom Murphy and Alfrec
in *The Visit* by Friedrich Dürrenmatt back in 1958."

PAULINE McLYNN

"There isn't one play that I would prefer not to have done... I think. Equally, I have too many friends in the business to choose one above any other – many of them know where I live... When I was a student I used to visit London every year to check out what theatre was going on over there. The biggest thrill was to see great shows but to know that we had as much talent in Ireland. I still feel that way. Tom Murphy is my favourite playwright. He writes gut-wrenching, life-changing plays and magnificent parts for actors. He is mischievous, thought provoking, maddening, funny and moving. Brilliant. And my parents are equally inspirational. They never bat an eyelid when I mentioned I wanted to give acting a go as a career. Perhaps they just didn't hear me properly."

MICK LALLY

"For a lot of my life I've been in shows that toured the country extensively and I spend my day in a very docile manner – I'm good at docility. It's always good to return home, to the Druid Theatre company in Galway. I really enjoyed doing Old Mahon in a Druid production of *The Playboy of the Western World* in the early 1980s, but I'll always be remembered for *Glenroe,* I suppose."

CANDY DEVINE

PERSONAL MANAGEMENT
DONALD McLEOD

CANDY DEVINE

SOLE REPRESENTATION
TREVOR KANE PROMOTIONS
DUBLIN 684442
BELFAST 21451

INGRID CRAIGIE

I love the National Theatre in London as a member of the audience. Over the years it keeps putting on all the plays I want to see. As an actor, it's got to be the Gate (Dublin) and the Royal Court (London) – both have a great sense of recent theatre history and intimacy. I met my partner and all my closest friends in various rehearsal rooms throughout my life. Before a performance I put photographs of family and loved ones around my dressing table mirror, it steadies me and keeps things in balance. And I rely on the wardrobe department for the best cups of tea, chat and gossip."

JIMMY O'DEA

"My grandfather, Jimmy O'Dea worked closely with all the names from the 1940s and 1950s – Vernon Hayden, Danny Cummins, Noel Purcell and more. But his most special relationship by far was with Maureen Potter, with whom he performed first in a production of *Jimmy and the Leprechaun* in 1939. They worked together hand-in-glove and brought out the best in each other. She was the perfect foil for him and credited him for teaching her all she knew about comedy and performance. He made *Darby O'Gill and the Little People* towards the end of his career, and despite an exciting shoot in Hollywood, apparently he couldn't wait to get back to Dublin for a decent pint."

Jennifer O'Dea on Jimmy O'Dea

MAUREEN POTTER

ADELE KING

"I know George Bernard Shaw had a very misogynistic attitude to women, but I love the English language and I adore what he does with it. John B Keane would also be up there with my favourites, as I don't think anyone captures the sardonic wit and the connivances and nuances of the average Irish man and woman like John B does. The Gaiety played such a pivotal role in my childhood and formative years, and I learned so much from watching Maureen Potter from the wings as a small girl. How do I unwind? I do tapestries, I read, I'm currently studying Latin, I take my beloved mutts for long runs down to the river, I listen to Lyric FM, I cook, and I'm a dedicated sugar crafter. I spend as much time as possible with my darling daughters and of course, I keep a watchful eye on my students at the Adele King Theatre School... after all, they are the stars of tomorrow."

PATRICK MASON

My favourite play is always the one I'm currently directing, and my favourite playwright is the one I'm currently working with. My preferred theatre is the one that's my current employer and I'm eternally grateful to everyone I work with for putting up with me. Theatre is the only business I've ever wanted to be involved in, but only God knows how I'll be remembered."

JEAN BUTLER

"Radio City is a special theatre for me. And the Project in Dublin. On a performance day, I like to arrive about three to four hours beforehand to prepare. I like to be in the theatre when no one else is there – it's a sacred time for me. My habits change with every performance but I always ask my gran up above to help me through. Success isn't something that's easy, and it's not going to be instant. You can never stop working at your craft."

MARTY WHELAN

"The Gaiety remains one of my favourite places. Beautiful interiors – the very epitome of the glory days of theatre. *John Player Tops* came from there, and my first foray into *Eurovision*. I believe in throwing myself into whatever I do – every day in this business is different and I'm still a big fan of meeting people from all areas. I love the variety of it all and while it's never steady, if you can live with that, it's fine. I hope I'll be remembered for spreading a decent helping of fun and love around. But truly, after a week, only those who loved me will remember."

"Some wise owl once said, 'The most important thing to remember about the saying "there's no business like show business", is that "business" is mentioned twice!'"

Stephen Brennan

STEPHEN BRENNAN
JANE BRENNAN
BARBARA BRENNAN

This photograph by Amelia Stein is from one of my favourite plays and productions, *Tis a Pity She's a Whore* by John Ford. A Jacobean tragedy, it was directed by Garry Hynes in the Druid Theatre in Galway in 1985. It boasted an extraordinary cast including Ciarán Hinds, Marie Mullen and Sean McGinley. Wonderful memories of our time together in Galway. That year, Druid premiered *Conversations on a Homecoming* and *Bailegangaire* both by Tom Murphy with Siobhan McKenna in the latter giving one of the greatest performances I've ever seen. Happy Days!"

Jane Brennan

"I love the plays of Tennessee Williams for his marvellous characters and enthralling writing; one of my favourite roles is Stella in *A Streetcar Named Desire*. I have numerous theatrical friends whom I've met along the way. I find with the most significant ones that even if not in touch for a while, we usually pick up from where we left off. My mother Daphne Carroll, was not only a wonderful mother, but also a brilliant actress and a huge influence on my life. I treasure a make-up box given to me by Alice Dalgarno when I played Sally Bowles in *Cabaret* – she was a choreographer and the first person I worked with in show business."

Barbara Brennan

ALICE DALGARNO

*To Eddie
Sincerely yours
Alice Dalgarno*

ANNA MANAHAN

"The Gate Theatre is responsible for so much of my professional life. I love its intimacy and its glamour and of course, I have very fond memories of Hilton Edwards and Michael MacLiammoir. Show business is unique in that it allows one to explore plays and share them with an audience. *The Rose Tattoo* is a particular favourite of mine and I loved playing the role of Serafina in that play. From an audience perspective, I found Donal McCann in *The Steward of Christendom* utterly memorable. Before I take the stage, I have a small statuette of Our Lady given to me by Francis O'Connor that I say a little prayer to."

ISOBEL MAHON

"I'll never forget the night I saw *The Plough and The Stars* at the Abbey in the 1970s, starring Cyril Cusack, Sinead Cusack and Siobhan McKenna. I was about twelve and I vowed from that moment I would become an actress. I met Mary McEvoy at the Gate a few years later, and the cast of *Glenroe,* who became like family afterwards. It's a privilege being able to bond with fellow actors and the audience over plays like my favourite, *Bailegangaire* by Tom Murphy. I still take it out and read passages for pleasure."

LOUISE STUDLEY

"The Gaiety was my 'home' for many years and I loved everything about it. I had an invaluable dresser called Annie who was my calming influence. And I would also rely very much on the musical director, who for many years in the Gaiety was Terry O'Connor. There's nothing to compare with the camaraderie of building a show from start to finish, and the excitement of an opening night."

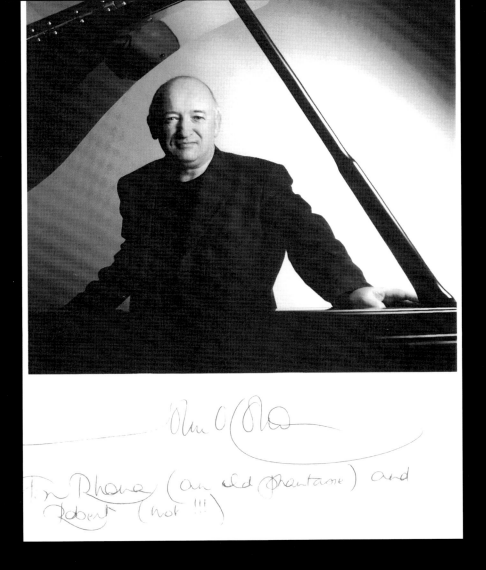

JOHN O'CONOR

"I have spent most of my life studying Beethoven and never tire of his works. I won the International Beethoven Piano Competition in Vienna in 1973 and since then he has been very good to me. I unwind straight after a performance with a nice meal and a good bottle of wine, preferably with good friends and ideally with my wife Mary. I wouldn't be where I am without her – she and I have been together on all major decisions in my life.

I've always loved the fact that the waiters in The Troc treat you well, even if you're a 'nobody' – and now I'm supposed to be a 'somebody' they still treat me the same. I'm delighted that my sons had the confidence to bring dates there for a special meal, knowing that they would be treated with respect, without knowing they were our children."

PAT LEAVY

"Pat Leavy will best be remembered as the smoking, croaky, loveable and loving grandmother Hannah Finnegan, mother of Rita Doyle in *Fair City,* until Pat's death in 2003. Always popular with audiences, I remember the one time Mayor of Carrigstown long before she filled the small screen with her matriarchal presence. She played a memorable Bessie Burgess in a production of *The Plough and The Stars*. Taking her cue from the text rather than tradition, she played the part as a truculent, striding northerner. Pat's death preceeded the smoking ban. Maybe she knew something."

Nial Matthews, Executive Producer, *Fair City*

PETER HANLY

"Show business is special, especially when you manage to overcome all the inherent insecurities that prevail, then it's a case of being paid for doing something you like, which can't be bad. The Troc is the real deal – it looks great, it serves great food and drink, but what makes it a true theatre restaurant is that it actually stays open late enough to accommodate theatre people who get out of work well past a sociable hour."

AISLING O'NEILL

"I have very fond memories of playing Slippy Helen in Martin McDonagh's *The Cripple of Inishmaan* in the Joseph Papp theatre, NYC. I have to admit I have inherited the various pre-performance superstitious rituals from my late father of turning around three times, tapping wood, muttering mantras and blessing myself – no wonder I need to get away from it all in my 'down time'. I love a day out on my horse, being around nature and then off to the pub for good times with good friends."

CHRIS O'NEILL

"Chris was happy in any theatre but some had special significance – the Abbey, where he trained as an actor; the Gate, where he was a member of the board; the Oscar, his very own theatre (briefly); any theatre his daughter Aisling was performing in, and the early days of the Project Arts Centre with the Sheridan brothers and a band of other lawless resolute. His performance as Vladimir in *Waiting for Godot* is one that's well remembered – a beautiful realised creation, poignant, vulnerable and achingly human. Chris was a loving father and loyal brother. A mischievous, adorable, impish, fun-loving rogue, a scamp, a scoundrel, a creative giant, a poet, a dreamer, a man for all seasons and a season for every woman. A lover of life and 'a darlin' man, Joxer, a darlin' man'."

Daughter Aisling and brother Vincent on Chris O'Neill

JOHN KAVANAGH

"I get completely immersed in the play I'm working on. I would normally start on it about a month before rehearsals actually begin. If I were to single out one part, it might be Joxer and that whole *Juno and the Paycock* experience. I love all theatre spaces, but I have a particular fondness for the London and New York playhouses. I spend a performance day preparing for that night's show and afterwards, when I get home, I like to sit with my dog and enjoy a nice glass of wine. On stage, though, it's achieving that special rapport with the audience which is so very, very satisfying."

TOM MURPHY

"Modesty forbids me from indulging in playwright accolades, although some recent Rough Magic work has impressed me a lot. I have very fond memories of The Trocadero since the Frank Harrison days, and of a one-off, late-night steak and kidney pie there about ten years ago. Robert Doggett is The Troc for me, and the singular kindness of all the staff. There's no better way of unwinding than with a bottle of wine, but I think if I were to only eat one more meal, I'd have to revisit that steak and kidney pie."

LYNNE PARKER

"When I was about twelve I saw Maggie Smith play Portia in
The Merchant of Venice on the BBC. I remember she made
this extraordinary poetry sound as if she was inventing it
there and then. My favourite play is also Shakespeare; one
I haven't directed yet – *King Lear*. I love the production part
of theatre, especially working with the designers on set,
costumes, lights and sound. I'm not superstitious, I live by
my instinct – if you don't genuinely believe at some point
that this is going to be the most disastrous show you've
ever done... then it won't be any good."

PAT LAFFAN

"Show business certainly beats working in the bank – I think – but I would advise anyone starting out to marry someone with good financial prospects!"

To Robert, — With love & thanks for wonderful food & service: & welcome, Virginia Kerr.

VIRGINIA KERR

'I owe a lot to Sister Peter Cronin, the marvellous nun who discovered I had a voice while I was in school at Mount Sackville Convent. Through my life I've treated it with respect and care. I have great memories of singing the role of Frau in Schoenberg's opera *Erwartung* at the Royal Opera House, Covent Garden in London which was terrifying but wonderful. Equally, I remember treading the boards of the Gaiety for countless concerts and operas there, hopefully there will be many more. Show business has a unique quality – we are all committed and enthusiastic and our common goal is to do a good show. I aspire to being remembered for singing wonderful music beautifully, and for my campaign to reinstate the warm chicken salad at The Troc."

MARY McEVOY

"I work in a business filled with great friends and one that gives me carte blanche to do the most ridiculous things – what's not to love? I'd like to say I'll be remembered for my role as Miss Julie, but I know it'll most likely be for being sent to my maker by a tractor."

"I want to marry Robert Doggett..."

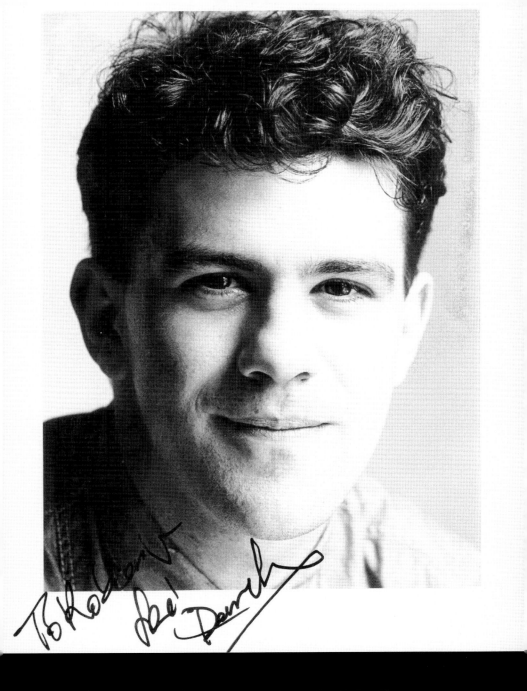

DARRAGH KELLY

"I graduated from Trinity in 1984 where I hung out with what would become the Rough Magic gang. We've all been friends throughout our adult lives. But my first and strongest influence would have to be my brother, Conor. We grew up together – he's a musician and an artist. When we were growing up I used to play music with him, and he'd act the maggot with me. We eventually got to work together in Rough Magic's *Improbable Frequency* and it was really special. I guess we have a bit of a mutual appreciation society thing going on."

FRANK KELLY

"I was very young when I first encountered The Trocadero, I'd say about 19 or 20. I was at the Gaiety playing in *The Heart's a Wonder,* which is the musical of *The Playboy of the Western World*. It was a magical place and I felt quite bohemian going up there to eat late at night. Everyone went there after first nights – maybe first to a bar, and then adjourn to The Troc. I can remember the late great American actor John McGiver, who starred in *Breakfast at Tiffany's* and *Midnight Cowboy* was very taken with the place. I can still see his big laconic face in situ... And that of George Matthews, a regular from all the early Paramount movies... It was very exciting to see people come and go when we were young. And of course, my wife, Bairbre – whom I met in a play – and I conducted our courtship there. It was, and still is, a moving gallery of famous faces going in and out."

MILO O'SHEA

"I have no favourite play, the special ones are like my children. Four of these would be *Mass Appeal* for which I received a Tony nomination on Broadway; *The Sunshine Boys,* because I got to work with one of my great friends David Kelly at the Gate; *Educating Rita,* because I got to work with my wife, Kitty Sullivan and of course, *Romeo and Juliet* in which I played Friar Laurence and which led me to a production for the BBC and then to reprieve the role in Zeffirelli's film of the same. My most memorable performance would be completely different, in the musical *Carrie* at the Gaiety. I had to dive through a window but at this particular performance, there was no mattress at the other side to break my fall, which I only noticed mid-flight. Thankfully, bruised and battered, I lived to take another dive. My best friend, and Troc dining buddy Paddy Guerin died of cancer 23 years ago. I'd like to dedicate this to him, and his wonderful wife Peggy."

BABS DE MONTE

To Eddie
Best wishes
from
Babs de Monte

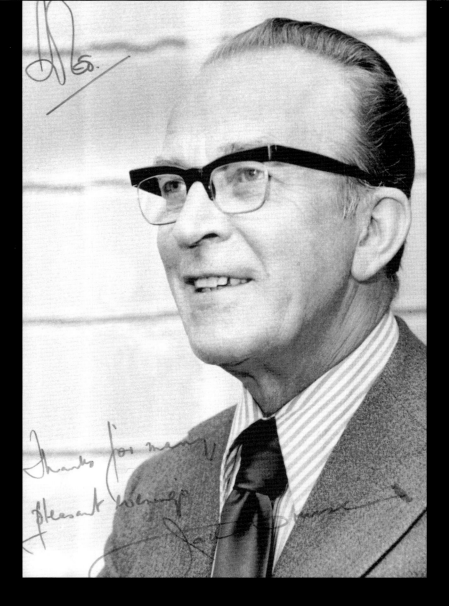

JACK CRUISE

"I think Jack will always be remembered in a peak cap, playing country man John Joe McHickey from Balaslabadasha Muckery, but I remember him fondly for his fundraising annual charity football matches at Dalymount Park – the Inkpots vs. the Crackpots – with fellow thespians and well known personalities. A keen sportsman and avid golfer, he was also a great friend to the likes of Noel Purcell, Frankie Howerd and Alma Carroll and liked nothing more than to relax in The Trocadero with his pals. He always said 'live every day as if it's your last, because some day you will be right'. He was a true man of his word."

Kevin Wall, Chief Barker, Variety Club of Ireland on Jack Cruise

DONAL McCANN

"I don't think Donal had a favourite theatre. For him, the part he was playing was all that mattered. He adored Friel's work and particularly the part of Frank in *Faith Healer*. I remember Donal's creative genius and the fun we had on so many wonderful productions. Just being on stage with him was an experience in itself and I wish he was still with us."

John Kavanagh on Donal McCann

NIAMH CUSACK

"My performance of Chekhov's *Three Sisters* is very dear to me. I did it back in 1990 with Sinead, Sorcha and Cyril, my father, at the Gate Theatre. Three sisters playing three sisters was pretty unusual, if not unique. And I met Finbar Lynch, my husband, on that job, so it was memorable on all fronts. I love the collaboration involved in theatre. I met Anna Mackmin, another person close to me, at an audition at the Royal Court in London. I told her I probably wasn't right for the part but that I'd love to play the character. She hired me and I've done some of my best work with her since. Amelia Bullmore, the writer and actress and another friend, is one of the funniest, most astute people I know. I do each show for someone I love/care about or admire."

SHAY HEALY

"The twists and turns of my life have been occasioned by chance rather than grand design. The luxury of hindsight allows me now to see that I set off without a compass and I also recognise the arc of my accomplishments has been too erratic to be called a trajectory. I found a bond with my theatreland friends because we were running away from reality – you do meet a better class of fantasist in show business. I've been a TV personality, a journalist, a radio presenter, a singer, a restaurateur, a magazine editor, a songwriter, a film-maker, a record producer, a recording artist, a novelist, a photographer, a playwright, a husband to Dymphna, a father to Oisin and Fionan, and a grandfather to Fionn and Nia. The Troc is my home from home."

GEMMA CRAVEN

"My most memorable performance has to be a production I was in of *Calamity Jane* – and never was anything more aptly named. It was so chaotic we never even got to do a dress rehearsal, so the first show was over four hours long. There were accidents before the interval, the sets fell apart, the horses' heads fell off – totally memorable! On first nights I get incredibly quiet and I don't like anyone around except my dresser. I'm not the ebullient person they see in rehearsal. The nerve situation is horrendous! I have to pretend it's not a first night, just a dress rehearsal with a lot more people. And as soon as I finish doing a play, the brain switches off and I forget everything. Come 4pm, though, I start to come to life again – it's theatre time. I don't think I was ever a morning person, not even when I was at school."

BOSCO HOGAN

"The Abbey Theatre is where I began my professional career. I'm deeply attached to it. It is my spiritual home. I have fondest memories of playing WB Yeats in the one-man show *I Am of Ireland: An Entertainment of WB Yeats* by Edward Callan on the occasion of the 50th anniversary of Yeats' death. The performance took place in the Peacock Theatre in the presence of the great poet's daughter and son, Anne and Michael. Also etched in my mind is playing Piper in *Observe the Sons of Ulster Marching Towards the Somme* in Belfast during a very tense political period. A young man of 18 came to me after one performance and confided that the play had been instrumental in persuading him not to join the IRA. God bless the spoken word and God bless Frank McGuinness. And I'll never forget taking over the role of Judge Danforth in *The Crucible* in the Abbey at 24 hours' notice. Such an adrenaline rush could not be bought!"

DEIRDRE DONNELLY

"My favourite play must be Shakespeare's Scottish play – you know the one! It's bad luck to say its name out loud. And for me, the Abbey Theatre is a very special place. Every time I work there, I meet the ghost of my 20-year-old self still walking the corridors. There, and in other theatres, I have met some of my closest friends through sharing dressing rooms. Away from audiences, Robert's welcome at The Troc is truly something unique, as is the atmosphere. It conjures up the feeling that you have all the time in the world to relax – which I love to do with a bellini and their heavenly roast breast of barbary duck on redcurrant gravy and onion marmalade."

FRANK McGUINNESS

"Work hard, write often, rewrite, believe nobody."

DEIRDRE O'KANE

"I'm a high energy person and I treat a performance day like any other. I do as much as I can – domestic stuff, shopping, washing, a voiceover, maybe even another job. Resting is useless for me and I don't like it. The more adrenaline pumping, the better. Energy begets energy, particularly with stand up – the more manic I am before a performance, that's the energy I go on stage with. I hate superstitions and good luck charms and I try to rebel against them. I've been known to mutter "good luck now, Macbeth" backstage, much to the annoyance of all. I rely hugely on my stage manager – their five minute call is when I get ready. And I love Robert at The Trocadero. He'll get you a table, even when you can't get arrested."

MARION O'DWYER

"I loved Arthur Miller's *The Crucible* which we did in the Abbey recently. It's everything a play should be; full of humanity and passion. The most craic I ever had doing a play was in Mark O'Rowe's *From Both Hips* for Fishamble Theatre Company. Impossible to choose a favourite playwright, but for carousing with, Frank McGuinness would be my playwright of choice. From the past, I love the language of Sean O'Casey, which is so satisfying to work on. I'd love to play Juno someday! After a show, there's nothing nicer than hooking up with a few friends and heading to The Troc, where you're bound to bump into a few more pals. I love my work, it's sometimes scary but it's always interesting; there's a sort of agony/ecstasy about the fear and the sense of achievement afterwards."

ULICK O'CONNOR

"I think Brian Friel is the nearest playwright to Chekhov that exists. He has interpreted Ireland for our generation by his incisive historical analyses and his astonishing ability to put characters on the stage who represent his themes. I, on the other hand, would like to be remembered for *Execution,* my play about the Irish Civil War and the fact that I was the first after Yeats to write successful plays in Noh form."

"The Trocadero's Dublin Bay sole is probably the best in the world, and is the best in The Trocadero when I can persuade the chef not to include onions."

"ONE OF THE GREATEST COMIC CREATIONS OF OUR DAY"
Financial Times

Paddy Wilson, Laurence Myers, Tom Kinninmont
and Independent Image Ltd present

PETER O'TOOLE

Jeffrey Bernard is Unwell

Written by
Keith Waterhouse
based on the life and writings
of Jeffrey Bernard
with
Royce Mills
Timothy Ackroyd
Sarah Berger
Annabel Leventon

Directed by
Ned Sherrin

Designed by
John Gunter

Lighting designed by
Simon Opie

48 PERFORMANCES ONLY

Best Comedy
Evening Standard Awards 1990

KATE O'TOOLE

"My first memory of The Troc is from the 1970s when it was far less salubrious than it is today. As a teenager I spent a 'gap year' living with the late, great Marie Kean, an old family friend who was always busy working at the Abbey. I'd often help her learn lines after which she'd reward me with a night out at The Trocadero where I'd always order the cannelloni. Since then, the room may have changed for the better, but the welcome could never be improved upon. The cannelloni is still on the menu and still tastes the same. The flaming sambuca has been discontinued, which is a shame, but knowing the clientele, probably quite wise."

DAVID KELLY

"Hugh Leonard is my favourite playwright, because he wrote great parts for me, also Chekhov, who didn't. The Gate Theatre feels like home for me, Michael MacLiammoir was an especially big influence on my career. Another great influence – and friend – is Jimmy O'Dea and I used to love The Troc (or Eddie Michaels' as we knew it then) in the early 1960s, when I think our photos were the only ones on the wall. Eddie looked after us well. As I remember, main courses at The Troc were five shillings. Mike Butts' Golden Orient was about the same for an Indian, and the famous Neary's salmon sandwich was half a crown. Bless The Troc, long may it welcome the poor, starving actor."

To Rhona,
With best wishes
and many thanks —
Olwen Fouéré

OLWEN FOUÉRÉ

"A typical day when I am performing means I sleep late, have breakfast in bed, do yoga, go to the theatre early, prepare for the show, get centred, listen for 'the call of the wild' and perform the show as though my life depends on it. Afterwards, I drink a glass or two of good wine with a small amount of food, hang out, go to bed late and sleep. Robert's personal specials at The Trocadero are unique and served always with love."

DERMOT MORGAN

Dermot Morgan was my father and I think about him every day. And each day his absence presents itself in different ways. But I remember him as a kind, beautiful, funny, complicated man who could quote a hell of a lot of Shakespeare. He always told us to write down our ideas, maybe that was the reason for the many green Pentel pens in his pockets. He had three sons, a partner, an ex-wife and an army of loved ones who still miss him greatly. Irish politicians, on the other hand, probably do not miss him, but they regularly make eejits of themselves in his memory.

Don Morgan on his father Dermot Morgan

BILLIE MORTON

"As an actress, and as the wife of Aonghus (TV and radio presenter), and mother of Aonghus Óg (actor) and Andy (an event manager), I'm living proof that show business is like malaria – it gets in the bloodstream. My favourite play is Sean O'Casey's *The Plough and The Stars* as every generation re-invents it. Bernard Farrell is a fascinating playwright; on first reading, his characters seem Irish, play them anywhere and you find they are universal. Before every performance, I make the sign of the cross – there are no atheists in the trenches!"

SIOBHAN McKENNA

"Jackie McGowan and Peter O'Toole were two of my mother's favourite actors – they were in *Juno and the Paycock* together. And of what she'd call the younger Abbey actors she had a great liking for Donal McCann and Niall Buggy. She also used to tell me the story of when Marilyn Monroe and Arthur Miller came to dinner. She asked Marilyn would she like to see her baby (me in bed). When Marilyn came down she said, "That's a man up there" – I was eleven. I slept through the whole visit and never even saw her. I have photographs of them together, which I treasure. I never realised that my mother was beautiful until I came across a photo of her taken when she filmed *Daughter of Darkness*. She looks so young."

Donnacha O'Dea on his mother Siobhan McKenna

For Robert

Down all the years, The Trocadero contains some of my happiest memories. Love, Phyllis Ryan.

PHYLLIS RYAN

"I went straight from school into professional theatre – it seemed quite natural to do at the time. The Gate will always have a special significance for me as I knew Michael MacLiammoir and Hilton Edwards well in my youth. I am fortunate to have made many good friends in theatre and get great satisfaction out of seeing their photographs all around The Trocadero. It becomes like another homeplace. I also like being served by a gentleman who looks like Hercule Poirot."